COLLECTIBLE MALE ACTION FIGURES

**Including
G.I. Joe ® Figures
Captain Action ® Figures
Ken ® Dolls**

By Paris and Susan Manos

COLLECTOR BOOKS

A Division of Schroeder Publishing Co., Inc.

The current values in this book should be used only as a guide. They are not intended to set prices, which vary from one section of the country to another. Auction prices, as well as dealer prices vary greatly and are effected by condition as well as demand.

Neither the authors nor the publisher assume responsibility for any losses that might be incurred as a result of consulting this guide.

The prices shown in this guide are derrived by the authors, wholly independent of Hasbro, Ideal, and Mattel and has no connection therewith.

This book makes reference to G. I. Joe®, Captain Action®, Ken®, and other identities for various figures produced by Hasbro, Ideal, and Mattel, which are trademarks of their respective manufacturers.

DEDICATION

This book is dedicated to Faith Wagner, a dear friend who has been a constant inspiration with "You can do it! You will do it!"

I Did It!

I would like to say a special thank you to Kevin Porter, my mentor and true friend who has always been willing to share with me his finds and who is fighting a battle of his own at this point in time.

Thank you
Edward J. Mokrzycki
For the inspiration on the
Ken® Doll Chapter.

Proofread by Roddy M. Garcia of
BACK IN TIME COLLECTIBLES.

INTRODUCTION

Collectible Male Action Figures

The need for information on collectible male action figures has grown over the past ten years. As male action figures and dolls become more collectible, the quest for information on this subject grows, and the need for qualified written material becomes greater.

No one can say that he is an expert in any segment of the world of collecting, as there is always something new and exciting a collector can discover about an item, no matter how many times it has been written about.

Collectors gather information in their own way. Be it through old store catalogs, magazines, or booklets, as they acquire more knowlege, they share it with other interested hobbyists.

I know for a fact, the more I learn, the more important it becomes to me to share my research facts. I find it gratifying to do this because in doing so, more and more join in on the excitement, and thus, the not too well known treasure gains recognition and becomes an artifact.

For this reason, I have gathered all my research and enthusiasm in this simple picture book "Collectible Male Action Figures."

G.I. Joe ® S.A.C. flight suit, flight jacket, and cap. Limited to 200 sets. Specially made for the 25th silver anniversary in Omaha, NE June 8,9,10, 1989. One given to each registered attendent. Valued at $200.00.

TABLE OF CONTENTS

CHAPTER 1

G.I. JOE®- AMERICA'S FIGHTING MAN FIGURES

From the beginning of time, boys played with toy soldiers. Archaeologists have unearthed small gold warrior figures and dolls from ancient Greek tombs where children were buried.

This manner of play has continued through the centuries. Boys as well as grown men are continually fascinated by war games. Many years ago, in a make-believe atmosphere, young boys would engage in battle with toy (cast metal) soldiers. Today, they play with combat ready, dressed action figures.

These play items through the generations have become highly collectible, not only with men, but with women as well.

This chapter will deal with G. I. Joe® action figures in combat and in adventure, by description and collectible value.

G.I.®JOE IDENTIFICATION MARKINGS AND DATES

1964

Marked on right, lower back:

G. I. Joe T. M. (Trademark)
Copyright 1964
By Hasbro R
Patent Pending
Made in U.S.A.

1965

Slight change In marking:

G.I. Joe R (Registered)
Copyright 1964
By Hasbro R
Patent Pending
Made In U.S.A .

This mark appears on all four branches of the armed services, excluding the black action figures. All figures have hard plastic heads.

1966

Same markings as 1965:

French Resistance Fighter
Japanese Imperial Soldier
Australian Jungle Fighter
German Soldier

These figures have hard plastic heads but no facial scars.

1967 - 1968 - 1969

Markings changed:

G.I. Joe R
Copyright 1964
By Hasbro R
Pat. No. 3,277,602
Made in U.S.A.

Heads are made of a semi-hard vinyl.
A talking mechanism was added to the line, with the exception of the black figures.

G.I. NURSE ®

Marked across back waist:

Patent Pending R
1967 Hasbro
Made in Hong Kong

Hard plastic jointed body and vinyl head.

1970 - 1975

Markings remained the same:

G. I. Joe R
Copyright 1964
By Hasbro R
Pat. no. 3,277,602
Made in U.S.A.

1975 - 1976

Markings changed:

c 1975 Hasbro R
Pat. Pend., Pawt. R. I.

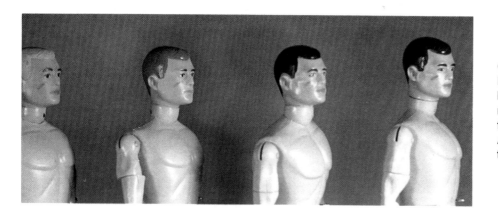

G.I. Joe® action figures came in four haircolors: blond, auburn, black, and brown. Each figure has a scar on the right cheek. These figures were sold in four basic packages: Action Soldier, Action Sailor, Action Marine, and Action Pilot.

As advertised in 1964, G.I. Joe® has 21 movable parts which enabled him to assume many action positions.

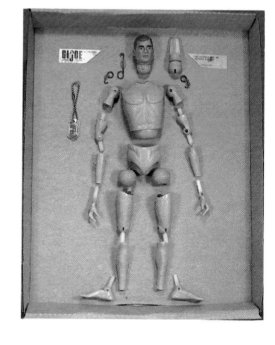

Action Soldier #7500 in realistic Army fatigues, cap, and brown jump boots. Also, training manual, G. I. Joe® dog tag, and set of insignias. Order catalog included. Assorted hair and eye colors.

Action Sailor #7600 in light blue denim work shirt, navy blue denim work pants, white Navy cap, and black boots. G.I. Joe®dog tag, Navy training manual and a set of insignias included. Assorted hair and eye colors.

Action Pilot #7800 in orange zippered jumpsuit, black boots, and fatigue cap. Also, Air Force training manual, set of insignias and G.I. Joe ® dog tag. Assorted hair and eye colors.

Action Marine #7700 in camouflaged fatigue shirt and pants with brown jump boots. Also, G.I. Joe ® dog tag, set of insignias, and Marine training manual. Assorted hair and eye colors.

Black Action Soldier #7500 in original fatigues. Black Action Soldier re-dressed in Marine camouflaged fatigues.

1966 Action Soldiers of The World. Members of this set may have any hair and eye color combination. These figures have no facial scar.

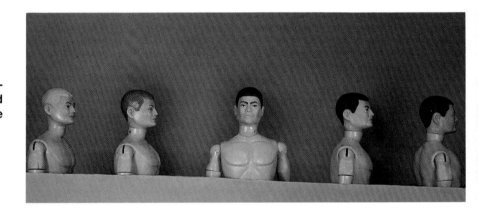

1966 French Resistance Fighter in black turtle neck sweater, blue denim pants with stitched simulated pockets (unlike sailor fatigue pants), and black vinyl beret.

1966 German Soldier.

1966 Japanese Imperial Soldier.

1966 British Commando.

1966 Russian Infantry Man.

1966 British and Canadian Commando. This is a rare and hard-to-find item. This figure was made by Hasbro of Canada.

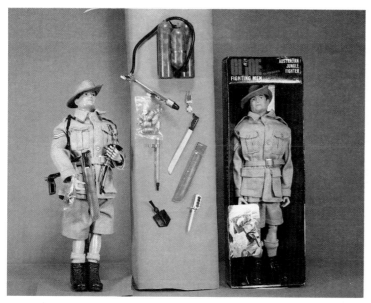

1966 Australian Jungle Fighter.

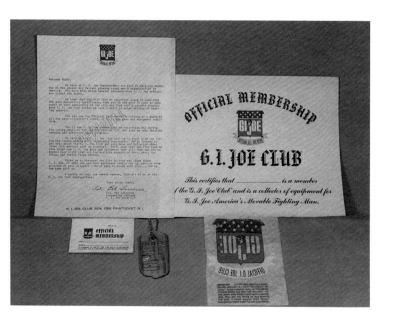

Official membership pack including welcome letter, membership certificate, life-size dog tag, membership card, and iron-on transfer.

1967 "America's Movable Fighting Man" talks.

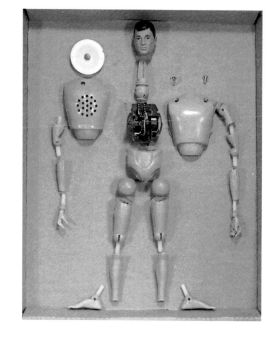

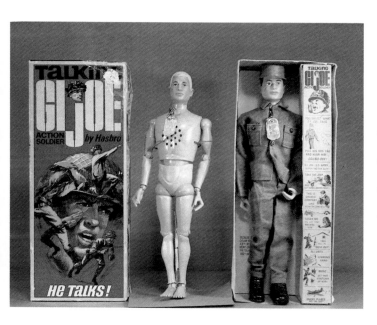

1967 Talking Action Soldiers.

Talking Action Marine.

Talking Action Pilot.

Talking Action Sailor (not photographed)

1969 Green Beret. Any hair and eye color.

1969 Green Beret.

1967 G.I. Nurse ®. The only female in this action series. Hard plastic jointed body, vinyl head with rooted short ash blond hair, and blue-green painted eyes.

1969 Talking Astronaut.
1966 Space Capsule Box.

CHAPTER 2

G.I. JOE® DRESSED FIGURES, UNIFORMS AND ACCESSORY PACKS

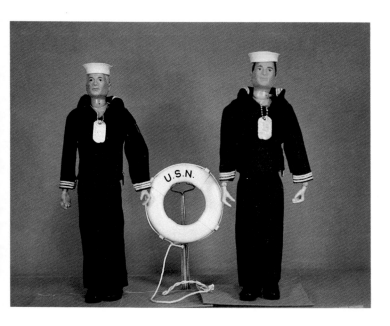

G. I. Joe® Sailor - Dress Uniform. First uniform mint and complete with dog tag.

Talking Sailor - Second uniform mint and complete.

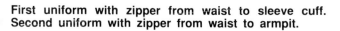

First uniform with zipper from waist to sleeve cuff. Second uniform with zipper from waist to armpit.

Combination Navy Attack Set #7607, plus Navy Attack Helmet Set #7610 shown on Action Sailor.

Rare Marine Jungle Fighter Set #7732.

(1) Arisaka Rifle and Bayonet (Japanese Soldier). (2) M 1 Rifle. (3) 45 Caliber Automatic Machine Gun. (4) Russian Infantry Man Machine Gun. (5) British Commando Sten Sub-Machine Gun and Clip. (6) M-60 Machine Gun. (7) White Dress Rifle. (8) Carbin and Bayonet. (9) French Resistance Fighter 7-65 Sub-Machine Gun. (10) German Soldier 9mm Schmeisse Pistol. (11) AR-15 Rifle. (12) AR-15 Jungle Fighter Rifle. (13) M-16 Rifle. (14) 40mm Grenade Launcher. (15) Machine Gun and Tripod (16) 81mm Mortar.

(17) German Soldier Grenades and Luger Pistol. (18) Automatic Pistol. Cal. 45. (19) Japanese Imperial Soldier Mamba Pistol. (20) Russian Anti-Tank Grenade. (21) Mortar Shells. (22) Underwater Dynamite. (23) Bazooka and Projectiles. (24) Hand Grenades.

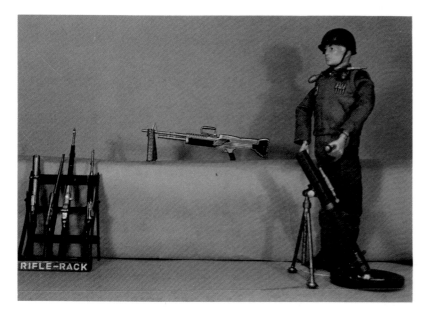

Weapons rack #7727 with M-60 and AR-15 rifles, carbine and 40mm Grenade Launcher. Heavy weapons Set #7538. 81mm Mortar with 3 shells, M-610 Machine Gun, Bi-Pod, Bullet Proof Vest with bullets and hand grenades, and 40-round ammunition belt.

Tank Commander Set #7731. Set includes an authentically-styled brown tanker jacket, tanker helmet, machine gun, tripod, ammo box, belt, radio, and tripod.

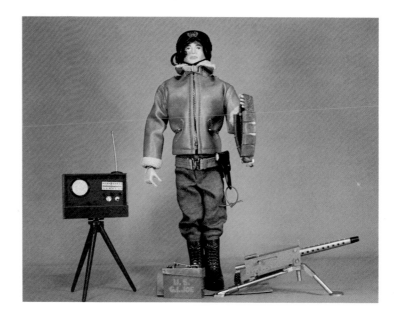

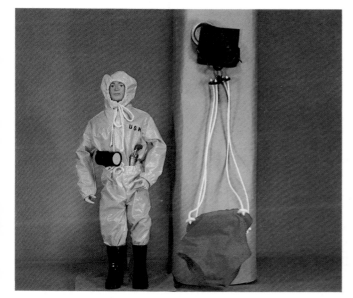

Breeches Buoy #7625. Set includes buoy, slicker jacket and pants, flare gun, blinker light.

Commando Outfit. Set includes raft with anchor and paddle, flare gun, blinker light, black knit stocking cap (hard to find), 45 caliber automatic machine gun, gas mask, wireless with earphone, TNT with detonator, and binoculars.

Communications Flag Set #7704. Flags for Army, Air Corps, Marines, and Navy, plus Old Glory.

Air Corps Dress Uniform #7803. Authentic Dress Uniform complete with dress blue jacket and Trousers, light blue shirt, tie and Garrison cap, plus wings and Captain's bars.

Air Cadet #7822. This set came in a photo covered box as well as an open cellophane covered box. (Photo boxed is more desirable).

West Point Cadet #7537. This set came photo boxed as well as in an open celo covered box. (printed box is more desirable).

Annapolis Cadet #7624. This set came boxed as shown or in an open celo covered box. (Printed box is more desirable).

Action Marine Dress Parade Set #7710. Includes authentically tailored dress jacket with brass buttons, trousers with red stripe sewn to sides, cap, belt, rifle, and Marine manual.

Action Marine. Sold through Sears Catalog in shipping box. Dressed in Dress Parade Set including dog tag, insignias, and Marine manual.

Military Police Set #7521. Authentic Ike jacket with ascot and pants in Army fabric, 45 pistol with holster, arm band, billy club, duffle bag, and Army manual. Helmet and accessories pack #7526 (not photographed)

Action Sailor "Shore Patrol Set"#7612. (not photographed). Includes dress jumper, pants, 45 pistol, white belt, cap, sea bag, billy stick, arm band, and neckerchief. These pieces also came in small individual packs (as shown).

Military Police #7539. Very rare turquoise Ike jacket with airborn emblem over left pocket, trousers, 45 pistol with holster, billy club, belt, black and gold helmet, radio, and arm band. This same set came in a light beige color as well and is equally as hard to find.

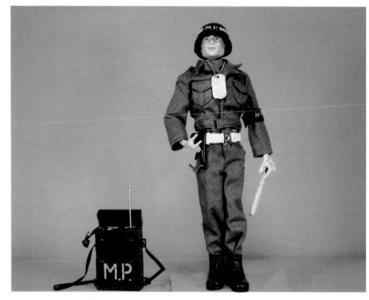

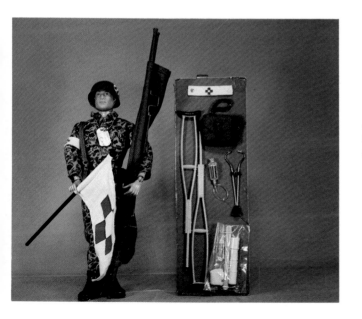

Action Marine Medic Set #7719. Includes stretcher, first-aid shoulder pouch, stethoscope, plasma bottle, bandages, red cross flag, splints, crutch, and arm bands.

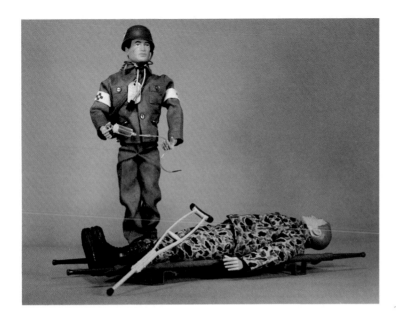

Action figures back from combat Medic and accessories.

Action Marine (as shown)

Action Pilot Set #7823. This set comes with an actual working parachute and pack, Mae-West life jacket, G-suit, crash helmet has face mask, hose connection, and tinted visor. Also included are flight coveralls, boots and flashlight.

Action Pilot Scramble set #7807. Includes authentic zippered flight suit, air vest, pistol belt with 45 and holster, and clip board with pad and pencil.

Small pack Scramble Crash Helmet #7810

Parachute pack #7811

Test Pilot Outfit also referred to as "Fantastic Freefall" from the adventures of G.I. Joe ®. Set includes, boots, orange coveralls, gold pilots helmet, Mae-West life vest, flashlight, working parachute and case, and blinker light.

Deck Commander Set #7621. Includes safety striped jump suit, cloth helmet with earphones, signal paddles, clip board with pad and pencil, binoculars, and flare gun.

Deep Sea Diver Set #7620. This set contains a waterproof suit, helmet with face mask that opens and closes, air pump with 24" long hoses, weighted belt, shoes, signal float, and deep sea hammer.

Astronaut Suit and Space Capsule. Actually designed from "Mercury Control" blue prints. Set includes a space suit made of fabric used by the real U.S. Astronauts. This set was used twice. First capsule has a blue interior, the second issue has a white interior.

Combat Engineer #7511. Set includes Engineer transit and tripod, helmet, and 45mm automatic machine gun.

Combat Construction Set #7572 includes Jack Hammer, construction helmet, and grey work gloves.

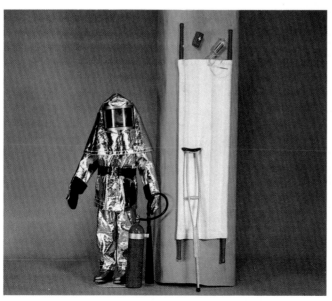

Fire Fighter Rescue Set. Includes real metallic heat suit with protective hood, gloves, boots, belt with handy accessories, chemical spray tank with nozzle, stretcher, first-aid kit, plasma bottle, and crutch.

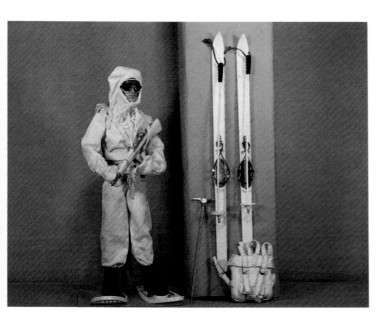

Mountain Troops Set #7530. Includes winter white camouflage pack, web belt, snowshoes, ice axe, climbing ropes, and grenades.

Ski Patrol Set #7531. Includes winter white camouflage, two-piece ski parka, boots, goggles, mittens, skis, and poles.

Frogman Underwater Demolition Set #7602. Includes rubber suit, headpiece, face mask, swim fins, scuba tank, knife, scabbard, depth gauge, and dynamite.

Deep Freeze Set. Includes fur parka, ski pants, ice boots, snow sled with tow rope, flare gun and ice pick.

Demolition Set. Includes mine detector, power pack, earphones, and mines.

These outfits were not distributed to all areas. They were packaged in plastic baggies. These outfits were very well made.

Police Officer

Race Car Driver

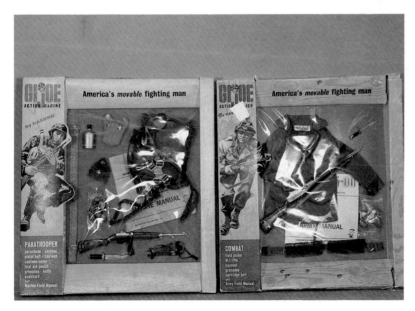

Combat Field Pack #7502.

Combat Field Jacket Set #7501.

Action Soldier-Bivouac Deluxe Pup Tent Set #7513.

Action Marine-Communications Post Poncho Set #7701.

Military Police Set #7521.

Marine Dress Parade Set #7710.

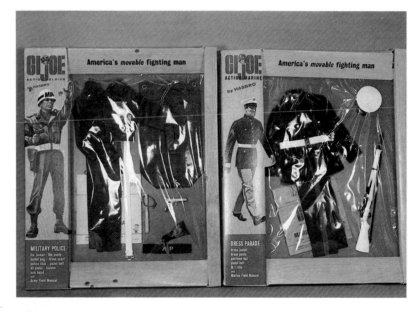

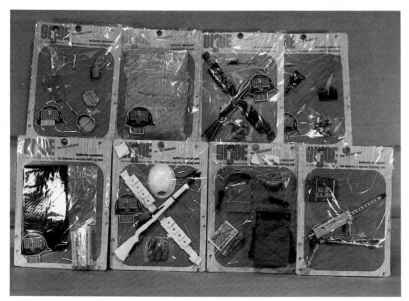

Assorted G.I. Joe ® - Action Soldier Packs.

29

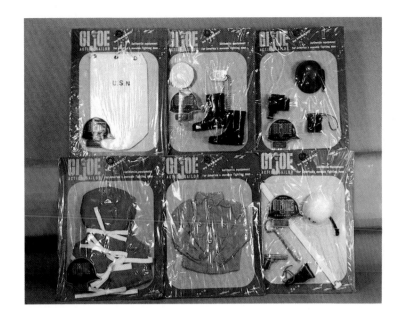

Assorted G.I. Joe ® Action Sailor Packs.

Assorted G. I. Joe ® Action Pilot Packs.

G.I. Joe ® Assorted Action Sailor Pack.

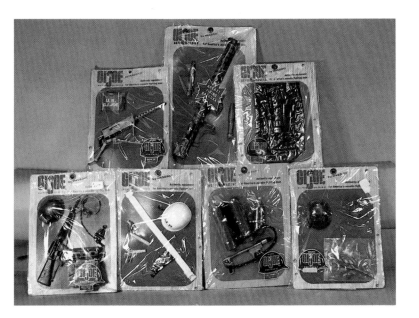

G. I. Joe ®Action Soldier Bazooka Pack.

Green Beret Pack

Assorted G.I. Joe® Action Marine Packs.

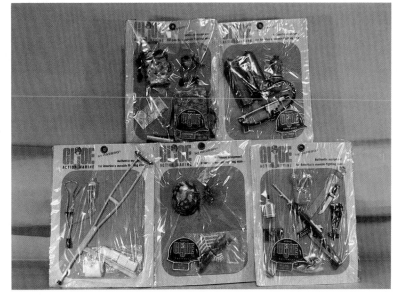

Special Offer: 4 Services in 1 Special. Accessories varied in count from 12 to 14 to 16 pieces, loose in plastic bag. Each set came with a 4 in 1 Comic Book.

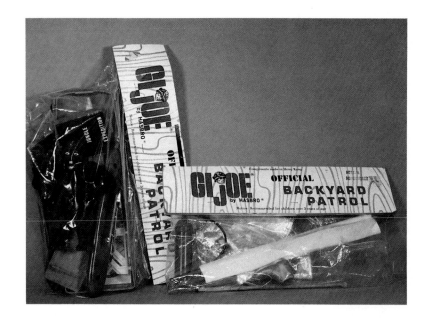

Backyard Patrol Sets.

Adventure Team Set

Crash Crew Set

Backyard Patrol Pack Sets.

Astronaut Suit   Astronaut Accessories Pack

Adventure Team Play Set

Astronaut Suit with Mine Sweeper

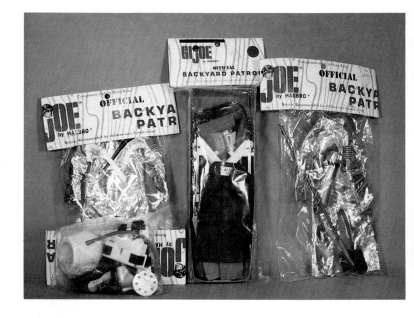

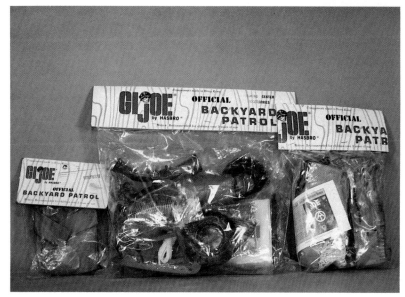

Backyard Patrol Japanese Soldier Suit and Helmet

Field Accessory Pack

Adventure Team Play Set

The Adventures of G. I. Joe® Underwater Diver Play Set.
The Eight Ropes of Danger.

The Adventures of G.I. Joe® Jungle Explorer. Figure included.
The Mouth of Doom.

The Adventures of G.I. Joe®Spaceman Play Set.
Hidden Missile Discovery.

The Adventures Of G.I. Joe ® Polar Explorer.
Figure included.
The Fight For Survival.

The Adventures of G.I. Joe ® Sea Adventure.
Figure included.
The Shark's Surprise.

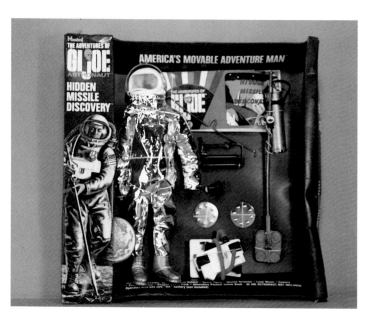

The Adventures of G.I. Joe ® Astronaut Hidden Missile Discovery.

The Adventures of G.I. Joe® Air Adventure Fantastic Freefall.

CHAPTER 3

ADVENTURE TEAM ERA
1970-1976

Adventure Team Membership Kit. Includes: Welcome letter, certificate of membership, dog tag and iron-on transfer and membership I.D. card (not shown).

G. I. Joe® Man of Action with insignias and dog tag like Action Soldier but Adventure Team Emblem on shirt.

The G.I. Joe® Adventure Team. Top Left: Black Adventures. Top Right: Air Adventures. Bottom: Left to Right, Talking Astronaut Sea Adventurer, Talking Team Commander, Land Adventurer.

Black Adventurer.

Talking Adventurer Team Commander.

Land Adventurer.

Sea Adventurer.

Air Adventurer.

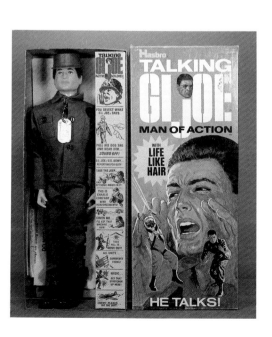

Talking Man of Action.

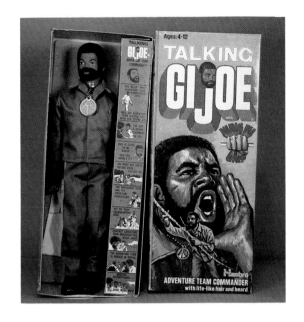

Black Talking G.I. Joe® with Kung Fu Grip.

Adventure Team G.I. Joe® with Kung Fu Grip.

Adventure Team G.I. Joe® with Kung Fung Grip.

Adventure Team. G.I. Joe® Black Adventurer with Kung-Fu Grip.

Eagle Eye G.I. Joe,® Land Commander.

Adventure Team Mike Power Atomic Man.

Bullet Man.

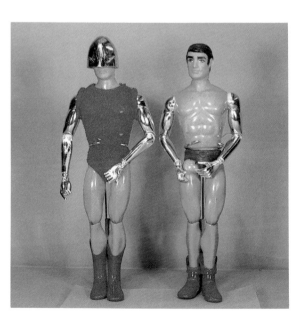

1977 Super Joe - 8¾"Tall. Made between 11½" G. I. Joe figure and 3½" figure on the current market.

Super Joe.

Super Joe Command Center.

Assorted Super Joe - Play Sets

Outfits

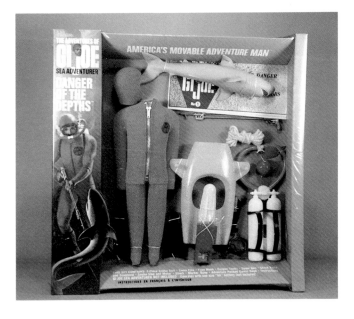

The Adventures of G.I. Joe® Sea Adventure. Danger of the Depths.

The Adventures of G. I. Joe,® Land Adventures. White Tiger Hunt.

Adventure Team, G.I. Joe ®- Jettison to Safety Play Set.

Adventure Team, G.I. Joe® Danger Ray Detection.

Adventure Team, G.I. Joe® Secret Agent.

Adventure Team, Radiation Detector.

Aerial Recon.

High Voltage Escape.

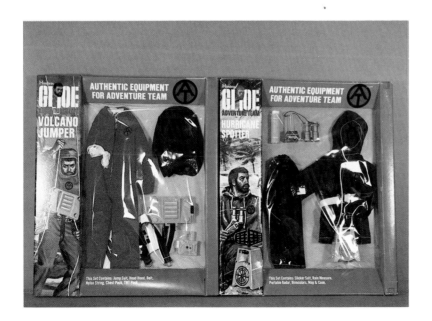

Adventure Team, G.I. Joe® Volcano Jumper.

Hurrican Spotter.

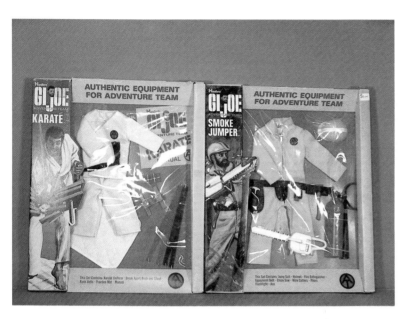

Adventure Team Karate.

Smoke Jumper.

Adventure Team, Jungle Survival.

Emergency Rescue .

Assorted Adventure Team Outfits.

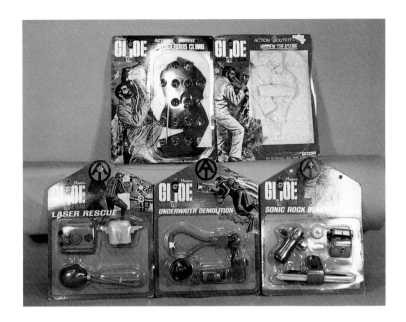

Adventure Team Outfits and Accessories.

CHAPTER 4

G.I. JOE® COMBAT
AND ADVENTURE TEAM VEHICLES

Friction - Powered Armored Car. 20" long.

G.I. Joe® Motorcycle and Side Car, by Irwin For Hasbro.

Desert Patrol Jeep #8030. With 50 Cal. Machine Gun. This vehicle came with a driver in Desert Campaign Hat and Uniform, Boots and "45" Pistol.

G.I. Joe ® **5 Star Jeep - #7000. With working 106 mm recoilless rifle, trailer and tripod, mounted searchlight and 4, 106mm Projectiles.**

Original Box showing Jeep and Trailer.

G.I. Joe® Official Sea Sled and Frogman.

G.I. Joe,® rare official Sea Sled and Cave, Frogman included. This set was a Sears exclusive. Sets sold elsewhere do not offer the cave.

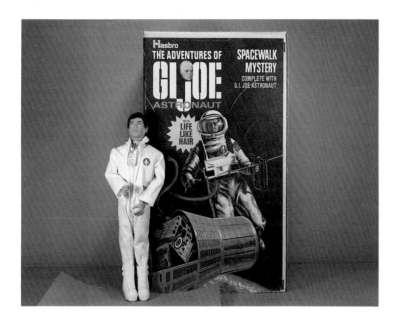

The Adventures of G.I. Joe ® Astronaut and Space Capsule. This is the Second Set. Space Capsule has white interior.

First Set had dark blue interior. First Set was offered by Sears and had a yellow colored Flotation Collar and Raft included.

This set is very rare and hard to find.

Other Vehicles not pictured.

G.I. Crash Crew Fire Truck.
G.I. Amphibian Duck.
G.I. Jet Helicopter.
G.I. Jet Fighter Plane styled after F-9F Panther Jet.
G.I. Carrier/Mine Sweeper.
This is a long Tank and Mine Sweeper attachment.

Jeep, part of J.C. Penny's Exclusive G.I. Joe ® Patrol Set.

Complete Set, includes Raft, Tent and Gear.

Adventure Team Vehicle, rides on land, floats in water. From the "Recovery of the Lost Mummy Set."

Adventure Team Turbo Swamp Craft.

Adventure Team Escape Car.

Adventure Team All Terrain Vehicle Play Set.

Adventure Team Helicopter, from "The Secret of the Stolen Idol".

Adventure Team Sea Wolf.

Adventure Team Big Trapper Vehicle.
Not pictured, G.I. Joe® Mobile Support Unit.

CHAPTER 5

G.I. JOE ®
COMBAT AND ADVENTURE TEAM
CASES AND TOYS

First G.I. Joe ® Official Foot Locker and Interior.

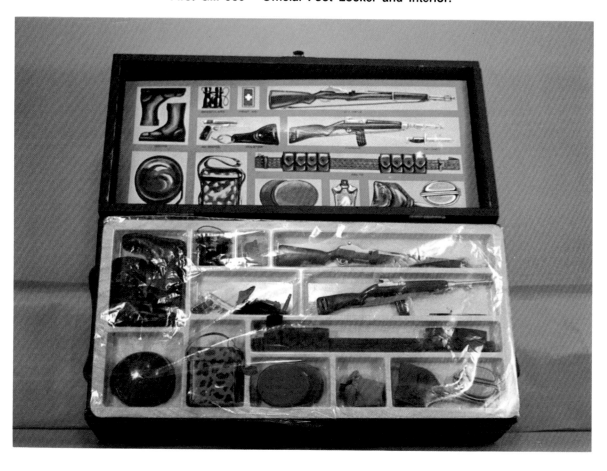

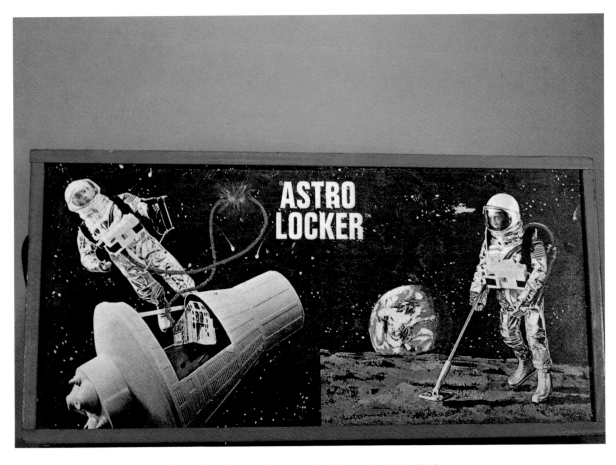

Astro Locker and Locker Interior. Hard to find.

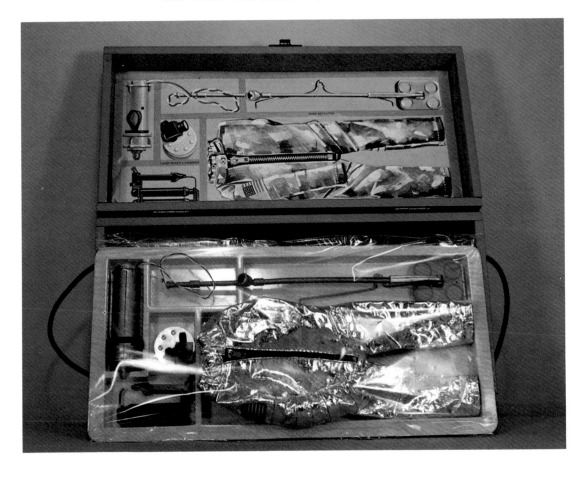

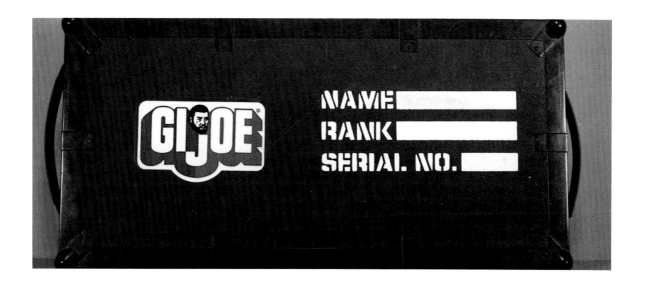

Adventure Team Foot Locker and Interior. Made of hard plastic.

Combat Man's Equipment Case.

G.I. Joe ® Bunk Bed.

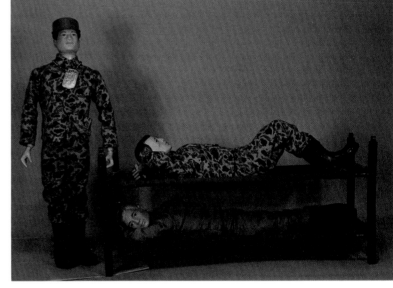

Child-Size Blinker Light.
Child-Size Canteen.
Child-Size Flare Gun.
Child-Size Mess Kit Set.
Child-Size Walkie Talkie Set.

G.I. Joe ® Metal Lunch Box.

G.I. Joe ® Electric Drawing Set.

G.I. Joe ® Combat Medic Kit.

Jumbo G.I. Joe® Action Pilot Coloring Book, over 300 pages by Watkins/Strathmore Co.

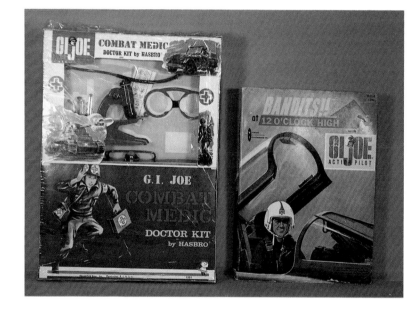

G.I. Joe® Action Soldier Coloring Book, by Watkins and Strathmore Co.

G.I. Joe® Sticker Fun Book by Whitman.

G.I. Joe® Coloring Book By Whitman-

G.I. Joe® Pencil Box, by Hasbro.

G.I. Joe® Jigsaw Puzzle.

Mess Kit.

Rare G.I. Joe® Watch, made by Gilbert. With compass and sighting lenses.

Child Size, G.I. Joe® Waterproof Poncho and Hood.

G.I. Joe® Bop Bag Punching Toy German Soldier, 51" high.

G.I. Joe® Adventure Team Colorform Set.

G.I. Joe® Adventure Team Dangerous Assignment Game.

G.I. Joe ® Adventure Team Small Book and Record Set.

Large Book and Record.

G.I. Joe ® Adventure Team Headquarters.

Not pictured, Mike Powers Outpost Headquarters.

CHAPTER 6

ACTION FIGURES FROM OTHER COUNTRIES

G.I. Joe[®] Action Figures were such a success in the U. S. that other companies around the world obtained the rights and licensing to produce their own line of Action Figures under different names.

Takara of Japan issued Combat Joe[®], Schildkrot of Germany issued Action Team,[®] Palitoy of England issued Action Man,[®] Other companies such as, Toltoys of Australia "Action Man".[®] Geyper of Spain, "Geyper-Man"[®] and Estrela of Brazil, "Falcon".[®]

This chapter will feature a sample of the Takara, Schildkrot and Palitoy line.

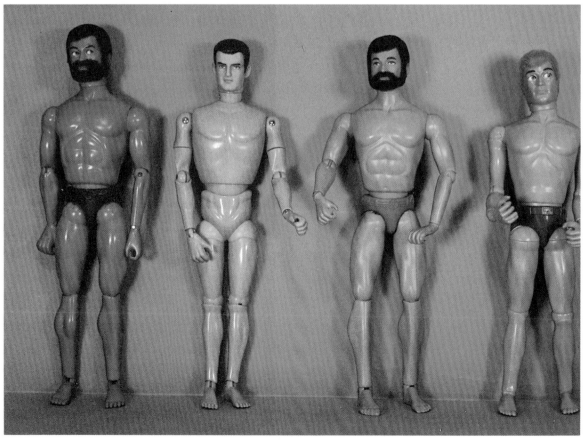

Last of U.S. Line. Adventure Team - Tamara of Japan, Schildkrot of Germany, Palitoy of England.

Takara of Japan - #1 W.W. II, dressed as American Soldier.

#2 W.W. II, dressed as German Soldier.

Takara of Japan - #3 W.W. II, dressed as U.S. Marine.

#4 W.W. II - dressed as German Officer.

Takara of Japan - #5, dressed as S.W.A.T.

#6 - dressed as German Tanker.

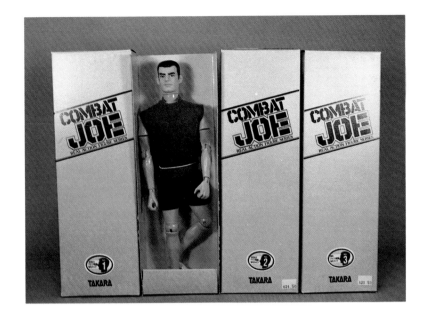

Takara of Japan. Basic figure. #1 Blonde, #2 Black, #3 Brown. These figures were sold to be dressed in special combat outfits.

Takara of Japan - Assorted Accessory Packs. Small Arms.
Carded Accessory Packs.

Takara of Japan Assorted Uniforms.

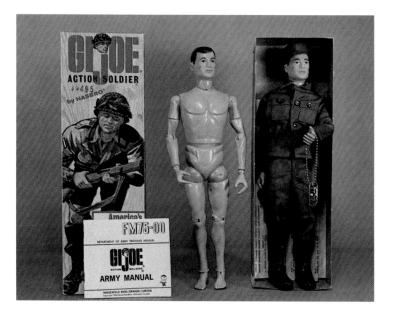

This G.I. Joe® was made by Hasbro of Canada and bears the markings, Made in Canada. A fine addition for any collection.

Schildkrot of Germany - Action Team Figure and Accessory Case.

Schildkrot of Germany - Action Team, Hard Rock Figure, first member of group of three.

Not pictured, 2nd member John Steel Figure.

3rd member Tom Stone Black Figure.

Schildkrot of Germany - Action Team Black Super Peggy Figure.

White Super Sandy Figure.

Schildkrot of Germany - Action Team Action Girl Ski Racing Outfit.

Schildkrot of Germany - Action Team, Action Girl Underwater Adventure Outfit.

Schildkrot of Germany - Action Team, Action Girl Safari Outfit.

Not pictured, Action Girl Parachute Adventure.

Schildkrot of Germany - Action Team Fire Fighter.

Schildkrot of Germany - Action Team Polar Adventure.

Schildkrot of Germany - Action Team Medic.

Schildkrot of Germany - Action Team Wilderness Adventure.

Schildkrot of Germany - Action Team Highway Police.

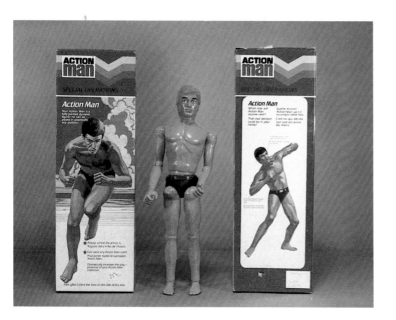

Palitoy of England - Basic Action Man Figure.

Palitoy of England - Action Man Soldier.

Talking Commander.

Palitoy of England - Action Man Helicopter Pilot.

Palitoy of England - Action Man Space Ranger Talking Commander.

Palitoy of England - Action Man Soldier.

Palitoy of England - Action Man Space Ranger Captain, Cloth Suit.

Palitoy of England - Action Man Space Ranger Captain, Rubber Suit.

Palitoy of England - Action Man Space Ranger Space Pirate.

Palitoy of England - Action Man Mounted Police.

Palitoy of England - Action Man. Action Soldier Engineer Pack.   Action Man Indian Brave.

Tsukuda Japan - Action Man, U.S. Marine Corps German Trooper, U.S. Army Green Beret.

Palitoy of England - Action Man Bunk Bed.

Special Operations Kit.

Rifle Rack and Guns.

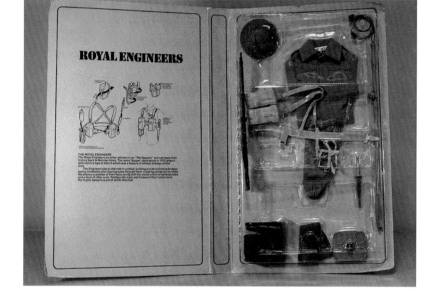

Palitoy of England - Action Man Royal Engineers.

Palitoy of England - Action Man, British Infantryman.

Mountain and Artic Outfit.

German Pilot Outfit.

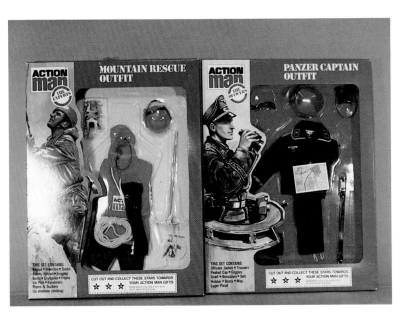

Palitoy Of England - Action Man Mountain Rescue.

Panzer Captain Outfit.

Palitoy of England - Action Frogman.

Royal Hussar

Palitoy Of England - Action Man Frogman Putfit.

Police Motorcyclist.

Palitoy of England - Action Man
German Armoured Car.

Palitoy of England - Action Man
Armoured Jeep.

Palitoy of England - Action Man
Helicopter.

Palitoy of England - Action Man Space Ranger.
Space Speeder.

CHAPTER 7

CAPTAIN ACTION® SUPER HERO

1966-1968

Captain Action® figures were created by the Ideal Toy Company and produced for a short time between 1966 and 1968. Not much is known about this exciting figure, but there is a lot of interest shown in this collectible.

Captain Action® represents a fictional character who assumes different identities by changing into many disguises. He is known as "The Amazing 9-in-1 Super Hero."

1 Superman	1966 c National Periodical Publication Inc.
2 Batman	1966 c National Periodical Publication Inc.
3 Aquaman	1966 c National Periodical Publication Inc.
4 Lone Ranger	Weather Corp. All Rights Reserved
5 Phantom	King Features Syndicate Inc.
6 Flash Gordon	King Features Syndicate Inc.
7 Sgt. Fury	Marvel Comics Group
8 Captain America	Marvel Comics Group
9 Steve Canyon	By Field Enterprise Inc.

Other characters added include: Tonto, Spiderman, and The Green Hornet.

Also Produced were Action Boy® figures (an 8½ inch figure) and Dr. Evil® figures (Captain Action's Enemy).

11½" Captain Action ® Figure: by Ideal Toy Corp.
Markings, back of neck: C Ideal Toy Corp. C M 1966.
Across upper back: C 1966 Ideal Toy Corp.

Captian Action ® 1967 Promo: Figure and 4 ft.
Parachute included in box.

Captain Action ® Superman Disguise and
Accessories.

Kripto, Superman's Dog.

Captain Action Figure ®(1966) in "The Phantom" Disguise.

Captain Action ® Figure (1966) in Captain America Disguise.

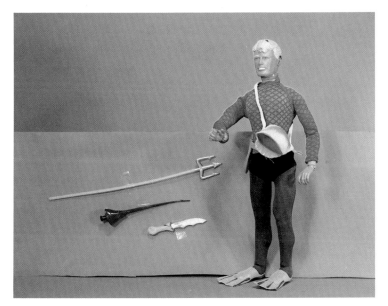

Captain Action ® Figure (1966) in Aquaman Disguise.

Captain Action® Figure in Batman Disguise. Some pieces missing.

Dr. Evil® Figure (Captain Action's Enemy) came with large number of disguises.

Captain Action® Flash Gordon Disguise.

Captain Action® Spiderman and Lone Ranger Disguises (in part).

Spiderman Outfit.

Lone Ranger Outfit.

Action Boy® Figure (not pictured) 1967, 9" Tall. Came in outfit same as Captain Action® Figure and Accessorized with knife, boomerang, utility belt, beret, and boots. His pet panther was a part of his original outfit, Action Boy. Mint and complete. Bits of original outfit plus pet panther pictured.

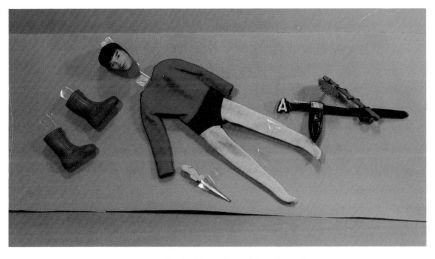

1967 Aqua Lad Disguise, Missing Spear.

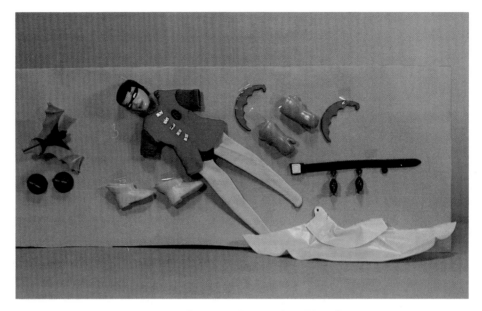

Action Boy   Figure 1967 - Robin Disguise.

ACCESSORIES NOT PHOTOGRAPHED

Silver Streak - Captain Action Car

Jet Mortar.

Weapons Arsenal with 10 piece set.

Action Cave (Vinyl carrying case) which converts to mysterious hide-away.

CHAPTER 8

KEN® DOLL AND FRIENDS "EVERYDAY LIFE"

Ken® Doll is a male fashion model produced by Mattel Inc. and introduced in 1961 as Barbie® Doll's friend.

Though he may have taken the sideline to make way for the ever-popular Barbie® Doll, Ken® Doll has made a mark of his own in the fashion world.

Ken® Doll represents the all-American boy, a young man that has had a college education and worked in almost every field from Fountain Boy to Astronaut. He is best known, however, as a male fashion model, who along with his friends has been very successful over the years.

This chapter will feature Ken® and Friends Fashion Models, complete wardrobes, and accessories.

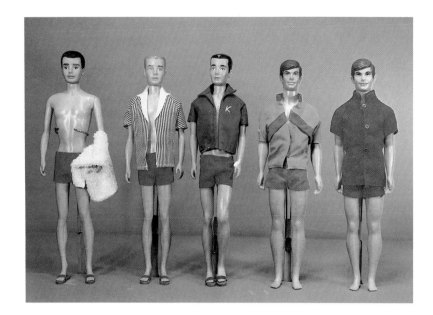

Ken ® Doll - (1961 - 1970)

Allen ® Doll - (1963 - 1964)

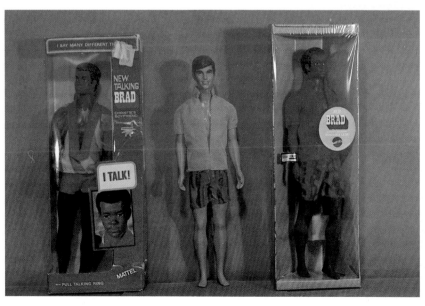

Talking Brad ® Doll - (1969)
Bendable (reg) (1971)
Bendable (reg) (1971)

Live Action Ken® **Doll on Stage (1971)**

Walk Lively Ken® **Doll**

Busy Ken® **Doll - (1972)**

Busy Talking Ken® **Doll - (1972)**

Mod Hair Ken® **Doll - (1973)**

Now Look Ken® **Doll - (1973)**

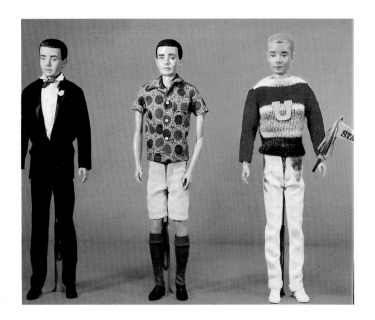

Ken® Tuxedo #787 - Jacket, trousers, dress shirt, black socks and shoes, maroon bow tie and cumberbund and white rose corsage.

Sport Shorts #783 - Sport shirt, Bermuda shorts, khaki socks and brown oxford shoes.

Campus Hero #770 - Sweater, white duck pants, red socks, white oxford shoes, "U" letter and banner.

Ken® Doll in Dreamboat #785 - Sport shirt and jacket, slacks, matching socks, black oxford shoes and straw hat.

Ken® Doll in Casuals #782 - Red sport hat, knit t-shirt, polished cotton pants, striped socks, 2-toned shoes and key chain and key.

Ken® Doll in Saturday Date #786 - Grey suit, long sleeve shirt, striped tie, black shoes and socks.

Ken® Doll in Terry Togs #784 - Terry robe, terry scuffs, soap, sponge, terry towel and wash cloth, knit briefs, electric shaver and comb.

Allen® Doll In Sleeper Set #781 - Striped P.J.'s, alarm clock, sugarbun and glass of milk.

Ken® Doll In "In Training" #780 - Knit t-shirt and briefs, boxer shorts, exercise manual and dumbell set.

Ken ® in "The Yachtsman" #789 - Denim sailing outfit, red striped t-shirt, black shoes, white socks and yachtsman book.

Allen ® in "Rally Day" #788 - Tailored beige poplin all-weather coat, red hat, map and car keys. (Slacks and shoes not included).

Ken ® in "Time For Tennis" #790 - White cardigan, white sport shorts and t-shirt, tennis shoes, socks, goggles, racquet and ball.

Allen ® in "Fun On Ice" #791 - Sweater, corduroy slacks, gold socks, cap, mittens, muffler and racing skates.

Ken ® in "Army and Airforce" #797 - Armed forces uniform with interchangeable accessories, beige cap, tie, belt, and socks, brown shoes. Also air wings, blue cap, tie and belt, black shoes and socks.

Ken ® Doll in "Play Ball" #792 - 2 pc. baseball uniform, regulation shoes, red socks, plastic hat, bat, ball and mitt.

Ken ® Doll in "Touchdown" #799 - Red football trousers and sweatshirt, red plastic shoulder guards, football helmet, socks, regulation shoes and socks and football.

Ken ® Doll in "Ski Champion" #798 - Red quilted jacket, knitted ski pants, stocking cap, mittens, ski boots, skis, ski poles and glasses.

Ken® Doll in "Red Riding Hood Wolf" #0880 - Checked cap, wolf mask, granny's nightcap. This is part of the set.

Ken® Doll in "Arabian Knights" #0774 - Red velvet coat, gold and white sash, gold turban, gold slacks, red velvet scuffs.

Ken® Doll in "Masquerade" #794 - Clown costume, mask, scull cap, clown hat, shoes and invitation.

Ken®Doll "Sailor" #796 - Authentic sailor suit and tie, gob cap, duffle bag, socks and black shoes.

Ken® Doll in "Dr. Ken" #793 - Dr. top and trousers, white shoes and socks, Dr. bag, surgeons mask and cap, stethescope and reflector head band.

Ken® Doll in "Graduation" #795 - Traditional black gown and mortar board and diploma.

Ken® Doll in "King Arthur" #0773 - Silver costume with red satin surcoat with gold belt, scabbard, sword, spurs, helmet and shield.

Ken® Doll in "The Prince" #0772 - Green and gold brocade jacket, white lace collar, velvet and gold knit tights, velvet cape, green velvet shoes, gold velvet cap, velvet pillow with glass slipper.

Allen® Doll in "Ken in Switzerland" #0776 - Grey shorts, red suspenders, white shirt, alpine hat, white knee socks, black boots, beer mug and pipe.

Ken® Doll in "Ken in Holland" #0777 - White long sleeved shirt, blue trousers, white knee socks, wooden shoes, blue cap, red paint kerchief and tulips.

Ken® Doll in "Ken in Hawaii" #1404 - Blue and white malu, yellow lei, sandals, straw hat, and ukelele.

Ken® Doll in "Ken in Mexico" #1404 - Brown coat and trousers, green cumberbund, white shirt, black bow tie, black boots and sombrero.

Ken® Doll in "Campus Corduroys" #1410 - Beige corduroy jacket and trousers. White shirt and red tie pack set.

Ken® Doll in "American Airlines Captain" #0779 - Authentic blue suit, captain's cap, black socks and shoes, white shirt, blue tie and flight log and duffel bag.

Ken® Doll in "Campus Hero" #0770 - Same as #770 - Same as #0770 (pictured on page 92) only with a letter "M" instead of the letter "U" Same value.

Allen® Doll in "Fountain Boy" #1407 - White jacket, white cap, tray with sodas, napkins, spoons, order book and two pencils.

Allen® Doll in "Roller Skate Date" #1405 - Argyle sweater, stocking cap, brown roller skates. Trousers not included in set.

Ken® Doll in "Victory Dance" #1411 - Blue blazer, white slacks, red vest, white shirt with red tie, red socks, black and white shoes.

Ken® in "The Yachtsman" #0789 - Denim slacks and jacket, red and white t-shirt, black shoes, white socks, white hat and yachtsman book.

Allen® in "Drum Major" #0775 - White jacket, red trousers, white plush hat, white socks and shoes and baton.

Ken® in "Special Date" #1401 - Navy suit, white long sleeve shirt, red tie, black shoes and socks.

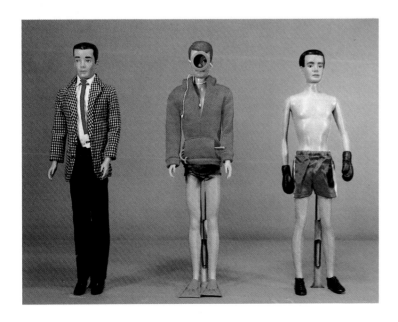

Ken® Doll in "Country Clubbin' " #1400 - Black and white check jacket, black slacks. Shirt, tie, shoes and socks were not included in this set.

Allen® Doll in "Ken Skin Diver" #1406 - Orange hooded sweat shirt, striped swim trunks, green fins, snorkel and mask.

Ken® Doll in "Boxer" (Pack) Blue trunks, boxing gloves, black gym shoes.

Ken® Doll in "Going Bowling" #1403 - Red shirt and grey slacks, (shoes and socks not included).

Allen® Doll in "Fraternity Meeting" #1408 - Brown slacks, white polo shirt, and brown and white cardigan, (shoes and socks not included).

Ken® Doll in "Goin Huntin'" #1409 - Red cap, red plaid shirt, blue jeans and boots, plus hunting gun.

Ken® Doll in "Cheerful Chef" Pack Set. Apron with forked hot-dog, spatula, spoon, chef's hat, red checked bandana and mitt.

Ken® Doll in "Mr. Astronaut" Silver space suit, brown gloves, space helmet, brown boots and the American Flag.

Allen® Doll in "Off to Bed" #1413 - White and blue knit pajamas, plush slippers, alarm clock, glass of milk, red telephone and book.

Allen® Doll in "Hiking Holiday" - Tan bermudas, green bulky sweater, brown shoes and white socks.

Allen® Doll in "Holiday" - Blue slacks, white knit shirt, white socks, black and white shoes.

Ken® Doll in "College Student" #1416 - Brown slacks, green and brown plaid jacket, white shirt, brown tie, shoes and socks, typewriter.

Allen® Doll in "Rovin' Reporter" #1417 - Navy blue slacks, red cardigan jacket, white shirt, black socks and shoes and camera.

Allen® Doll in "Best Man" #1425 - White dress jacket. black trousers, white dress shirt, red cumberbund, and bow tie, black socks and shoes.

Allen® Doll in "Jazz Concert" #1420 - Tan and blue short sleeve sweater, shirt, tan trousers. White socks and white tennis shoes.

Allen® Doll in "Seein' The Sights" #1421 - Red and navy tweed jacket, navy blue slacks, white long sleeve shirt, red tie, black shoes and socks.

Ken® Doll in "Here Comes The Groom" #1426 - Grey dress coat (with tails), grey and white striped trousers, white high collar dress shirt, light grey vest, grey ascot tie, light grey suede gloves, black shoes and socks, and light grey top hat. Very rare.

Ken® Doll in "T.V.'s Good Tonight" #1419 - Red monogrammed robe, red scuffs, and portable TV set.

Ken® Doll in "Summer Job" #1422 - Grey jacket and trousers, moss green and white striped long sleeve shirt, moss green tie, black shoes and socks. Hard to find.

Allen® Doll in "Ken A GO GO" #1423 - Red, gold and green striped shirt, gold slacks, fake black fur wig, white socks, and tennis shoes, gold ukulele and strap, and microphone.

Ken® Doll in "Time to Turn In" #1418 - Navy blue and red polka dot pajama and electric razor.

Ken ® Doll in "Business Appointment" #1424 - Black and white tweed overcoat, black felt humberg hat, black leather type gloves, black brief case and Mattel Daily News Paper, (suit not included), hardest of all Ken's outfits to find, very rare.

Assorted Ken ® Packs.

Ken ® Doll returns after a two year sabbatical. He now talks and shows signs of maturing.

Ken ® Doll in "Rally Gear" #1429 - Leatherette Jacket, gold duck slacks, gold, orange and blue striped shirt, brown high boots.

Brad ® Doll, Ken ® Doll's new friend in "Town Turtle" #1430 Turtle neck dickie, blue sport jacket, blue and grey bell bottom slacks, black loafers.

Brad ® Doll in "Groovy Formal" - Red Marou jacket, white long sleeve ascot shirt, gold and red brocade vest, white shoes.

Ken® Doll in "Play It Cool" #1433 - Gold felt jacket, gold and black plaid slacks, red turtle-neck pullover, brown loafers.

Ken® Doll in "Big Business" #1434 - Black and white check suit, turquoise shirt, striped pink tie and black loafers.

Ken® Doll in "Bold Gold" #1436 - Gold turtle-neck pullover, orange and gold plaid sport jacket, gold slacks, gold socks and brown shoes.

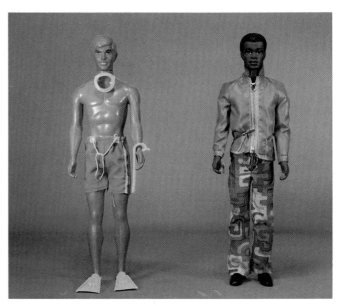

Ken® Doll and Brad in "Shore Lines" #1435 - (2 in 1 set) Ken in turquoise and gold swim trunks, face mask, snorkle and swim fins. Brad in turquoise zippered slicker jacket and multi-colored slacks. (Shoes not included in set).

Not pictured. Ken Doll's "Breakfast at 7" #1428 - Orange and gold robe and belt. Gold and orange plaid pajamas. Brown leather type scuffs and electic razor.

Ken® Doll in "Sea Scene" #1449 - Red, white and blue striped zippered jacket and slacks, blue turtle-neck dickie, white belt (not pictured), this set came with two different sets of shoes. One set with white beach sandals, other set with blue and white tennis shoes.

Ken® Doll in "Casual Scene" #1472 - Blue felt short coat, blue and red knit slacks, white dickie, blue socks and black shoes.

Brad® Doll in "V.I.P. Scene" #1473 - Red and black plaid suit, red short sleeve shirt, white tie, black socks and shoes.

Ken® Doll in "Ski-ing Scene" #1438 - Gold, red and blue striped turtle-neck pullover ski sweater with matching ski cap. Navy blue slacks, black shoes and socks, skis and poles.

Ken® Doll in "Suede Scene" #1439 - Suede trousers, red and gold print long sleeve shirt, gold socks and shoes.

Ken® Doll in "Night Scene" #1496 - Wine colored velveteen dress jacket trimmed with satin, velveteen trousers, satin cumberbund. White ruffled front dickie with black bow tie, black socks and shoes.

Malibu Ken® Gift Set - "Surf's In". This is the only gift set offered just for Ken.

Ken's® "Hot Rod" Hard to find in fine condition.

**Ken's® Wardrobe Closet - Made by Suzie Goose.
Licensed by Mattel.**

Child - Size Vinyl and Foam throw pillow.

First Ken [®] Case - 1961. Made in assorted colors.

Second Ken [®] Case - 1963, Made in assorted colors.

Ken [®] and Allen [®] Case. Sold only in France.

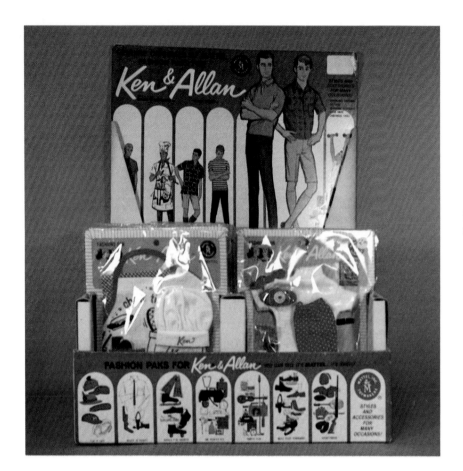

Ken® and Allen® Dolls. Pack Set Display, plus assorted packs.

Ken® Pattern Display, by Advance. Holds six pattern packs.

PRICING GUIDE

Pricing in this book is based on Mint-In-Box (M.I.B.), Mint-In-Package (M.I.P.), Mint-On-Card (M.O.C.) and mint condition items.

Pricing beyond this scale is left to the discretion of the individual.

Chapter 1

G.I. JOE® - AMERICA'S FIGHTING MAN FIGURES

Page 8
Action Soldier #7500
Figure $125.00

Page 9
Action Sailor #7600
Figure $125.00
Action Marine #7700
Figure $125.00
Action Pilot #7800
Figure $150.00

Page 10
Black Action Soldier #7500
Figure $500.00
Figure ....(out of box) $150.00 to $300.00
1966 French Resistance Fighter
Figure $250.00
Accessories Pack $50.00
Figure with Accessories $350.00

Page 11
1966 German Soldier
Figure $50.00
Accessories $50.00
Figure with Accessories $350.00
1966 Japanese Imperial Soldier
Figure $250.00
Accessories Pack $75.00
Figure with Accessories $400.00
1966 British Commando
Figure $250.00
Accessories Pack $50.00
Figure with Accessories $350.00

Page 12
1966 Russian Infantry Man
Figure $250.00
Accessories Pack $50.00
Figure with Accessories $400.00
1966 British and Canadian Command
Figure $400.00
1966 Australian Jungle Fighter
Figure $250.00
Accessories Pack $50.00
Figure with Accessories $400.00

Page 13
Official Membership Pack
Unused $20.00
1967 Talking Action Soldiers
Figure $175.00
Talking Action Marine
Figure $200.00
Talking Action Pilot $200.00
Talking Action Sailor
Figure $175.00

Page 14
1969 Green Beret
Figure $200.00
Figure with Accessories $300.00
1969 Green Beret
Figure (out of box) ....$150.00 to $175.00
Buzooka Pack $50.00
1967 G.I. Nurse®
Figure ....$500.00 and up

Page 15
1969 Talking Astronaut
Figure $200.00

Chapter 2

G.I. JOE® DRESSED FIGURES, UNIFORMS AND ACCESSORY PACKS

Page17
G.I. Joe® Sailor - Dress Uniform
Figure ....$100.00 and up
Talking Sailor ....$125.00 and up
Combination Navy Attack Set #7607 plus Navy Attack Helmet
Set #7610 ....$100.00 and up

Page 18
Rare Marine Jungle Fighter Set #7732 ....$200.00 and up

Page 19
Weapons Rack #7727 ....$40.00 and up
Heavy Weapons Set #7538
With Figure ....$195.00 and up
Tank Commander Set #7731
With Figure ....$175.00 and up
Breeches Buoy #7625
With Figure ....$175.00 and up

Page 20
Commando Outfit
With Figure ....$200.00 and up
Communications Flag Set #7704
(in or out of packaging) ....$70.00 and up
Air Corps Dress Uniform #7803
With Figure ....$175.00 and up
Air Cadet #7822
With Figure $150.00
Photo Boxed $225.00
Celo Covered Box ....$100.00 and up

Page 21
West Point Cadet #7537
With Figure $150.00
Photo Boxed $225.00
Open Front Boxed ....$100.00 and up
Annapolis Cadet #7624
With Figure $175.00
Photo Boxed $250.00
Open Front Box ....$100.00 and up

Page 22
Action Marine Dress Parade Set #7710 ....$100.00

Chapter 2 (continued)

With Figure $125.00
Action Marine Figure $200.00
Military Police Set #7521 .... $100.00
Helmet and Accessories Pack #7526 .... $40.00
    With Figure $125.00

Page 23

Action Sailor "Shore Patrol Set" #7612 .... $100.00
    With Figure $125.00
Military Police Set #7539 .... $250.00
    With Figure $225.00
Action Marine Medic Set #7719 .... $100.00
    Individual Packs $40.00
    With Figure $125.00

Page 24

Medic and Accessories .... $150.00 and up
Action Marine $60.00
Action Pilot Set #7807 .... $150.00
    With Figure $175.00
Action Pilot Scramble Set #7807 .... $100.00
Small Pack Scramble Crash Helmet #7810 .... $20.00
Parachute Pack #7811 .... $20.00
    With Figure .... $125.00 and up

Page 25

Test Pilot Outfit
    With Figure .... $175.00 and up
Deck Commander Set #7621 .... $100.00
    Pack Set $50.00
    With Figure. .... $125.00 and up
    Deep Sea Diver Set #7620 .... $100.00
    On Figure .... $125.00 and up

Page 26

Astronaut Suit and Space Capsule ...... $60.00 and up
    Dressed Figure $125.00
Combat Engineer Set #7511
    Dressed Figure and Set .... $175.00 and up
Combat Construction Set #7572
    Pack Set .... $75.00 and up
    With Figure .... $125.00 and up
Fire Fighter Rescue Set
    Dressed Figure with Accessories .... $175.00 and up

Page 27

Mountain Troops Set #7530 .... $65.00
Ski Patrol Set #7531 .... $100.00
    With Figure .... $125.00 and up
Frogman Underwater Demolition Set #7602 .... $100.00
    Individual Pack Pieces .... $30.00 and up
    Dressed Figure .... $125.00 and up
Deep Freeze Set .... $175.00 and up

Page 28

Demolition Set $75.00
    With Dressed Figure .... $125.00 and up
Police Officer .... $150.00 and up
Race Car Driver .... $100.00 and up
Combat Field Pack #7502 .... $35.00
Combat Field Jacket Set #7501 .... $45.00

Page 29

Action Soldier-Bivouac Deluxe Pup Tent Set #7513 ..... $100.00
Communications Post Poncho Set #7701 .... $100.00
Military Police Set #7521 .... $100.00
Marine Dress Parade Set #7710 .... $100.00
G.I. Joe® Action Soldier Packs .... (Each) $25.00 to $35.00

Page 30

G.I. Joe® Action Sailor Packs .... (Each) $25.00 to $35.00
G.I. Joe® Action Marine Packs .... (Each) $25.00 to $40.00
G.I. Joe® Action Sailor Pack .... (Each) $35.00 to $45.00

Page 31

G.I. Joe® Action Soldier Bazooka Pack $65.00
Green Beret Pack $60.00
All Others .... (Each) $35.00 to $45.00
G.I. Joe® Action Soldier Packs .... (Each) $25.00 to $40.00

Page 32

Adventure Team Set $50.00
Crash Crew Set $75.00
Backyard Patrol Pack Sets
Astronaut Suit $20.00
Astronaut Accessories Pack $20.00
Adventure Team Play Set $50.00
Astronaut Suit with Mine Sweeper $60.00
Backyard Patrol Japanese Soldier Suit and Helmet $20.00
Field Accessory Pack $45.00
Adventure Team Play Set $45.00

Page 33

G.I. Joe® Underwater Diver Play Set $165.00
G.I. Joe® Jungle Explorer $225.00
G.I. Joe® Spaceman Play Set $165.00

Page 34

G.I. Joe® Polar Explorer $250.00
G.I. Joe® Sea Adventure $225.00

Page 35

G.I. Joe® Astronaut Hidden Missile Discovery $150.00
G.I. Joe® Air Adventure Fantastic Freefall $150.00

Chapter 3
ADVENTURE TEAM ERA

Page 37

Adventure Team Membership Kit $25.00
G.I. Joe® Man of Action $100.00

Page 38

    G.I. Joe® Adventure Team
    Black Adventurer $125.00
    Talking Adventurer Team Commander $125.00
    Land Adventurer $100.00

Page 39

    Sea Adventurer $100.00
    Air Adventurer $100.00
    Talking Man of Action $125.00

Page 40
Black Talking G.I. Joe® with Kung Fu Grip $150.00
Adventure Team G.I. Joe®with Kung Fu Grip $100.00
Adventure Team G.I. Joe® with Kung Fu Grip $100.00

Page 41
Adventure Team G.I. Joe®Black Adventurer with Kung-Fu Grip
    Figure $75.00
Eagle Eye G. I. Joe®, Land Commander $65.00
Adventure Team Mike Power Atomic Man
    Figure $65.00
    Figure ....$15.00 (out of Packaging)
Bullet Man $60.00

Page 42
1977 Super Joe $25.00
Super Joe $25.00
Super Joe Command Center....................$15.00 and up
Assorted Super Joe
    Play Sets ....(Each) $15.00
    Outfits ....(Each) $10.00
Danger of the Depths $150.00

Page 43
Land Adventures. White Tiger Hunt $125.00
Danger Ray Detection $35.00

Page 44
Secret Agent $45.00
Radiation Detector $30.00
Aerial Recon $30.00
High Voltage Escape $30.00
Volcano Jumper $30.00
Hurricane Spotter $30.00

Page 45
Adventure Team Karate $30.00
Smoke Jumper $30.00
Adventure Team Jungle Survival $35.00
Emergency Rescue $35.00
Assorted Adventure Team Outfits ....(Each) $70.00

Page 46
Adventure Team Outfits and Accessories ....(Each) $7.00

Chapter 4
G.I. JOE® COMBAT
AND ADVENTURE TEAM VEHICLES

Page 48
Friction - Powered Armored Car ....$75.00 and up

Page 49
G.I. Joe® Motorcycle and Side Car ....$75.00 and up

Page 50
Desert Patrol Jeep #8030 ....$200.00

Page 51
G.I. Joe® 5 Star Jeep #7000 ....$100.00 and up

Page 52
G.I. Joe® Official Sea Sled and Frogman ....$100.00 and up

Page 53
G.I. Joe® rare official Sea Sled and Cave ......$150.00 and up

Page 54
Astronaut and Space Capsule
    Second Set ....$175.00 and up
    First Set ....$175.00 and up
    Both Sets ....$250.00 and up
    Flotation Collar ....$50.00 and up
G.I. Crash Crew Fire Truck ....$150.00 and up
G.I. Amphibian Duck ....$200.00 and up
G.I. Jet Helicopter ....$200.00 and up
G.I. Military Staff Car ....$100.00 and up
G.I. Carrier/Mine Sweeper ....$200.00 and up
J.C. Penney's Patrol Set Jeep ....$50.00 and up
    Complete Set ....$150.00 and up

Page 55
Adventure Team Vehicle ....$150.00 and up
Adventure Team Turbo Swamp Craft ....$50.00 and up
Adventure Team Escape Car ....$15.00 and up

Page 56
All Terrain Vehicle Play Set ....$75.00 and up
Adventure Team Helicopter $30.00
    Play Set ....$50.00 and up

Page 57
Adventure Team Sea Wolf ....$40.00 and up
Adventure Team Big Trapper Vehicle ....$45.00 and up
Mobile Support Unit $75.00

Chapter 5
G.I. JOE®
COMBAT AND ADVENTURE TEAM
CASES AND TOYS

Page 59
Foot Locker and Interior
    Locker Only ....(Unplayed Condition) $35.00

Page 60
Astro Locker and Locker Interior ....$50.00 and up

Page 61
Adventure Team Foot Locker and Interior ....$15.00 and up

Page 62
Combat Man's Equipment Case ....$15.00 and up
G.I. Joe® Bunk Bed ....$20.00 and up
Child-Size Blinker Light Set ....$15.00 and up
Child-Size Canteen ....$5.00 and up
Child-Size Flare Gun ....$5.00 and up
Child-Size Mess Ket Set ....$10.00 and up
Child-Size Walkie Talkie Set ....$15.00 and up

Page 63
G.I. Joe® Metal Lunch Box ....$10.00 and up
G.I. Joe® Electric Drawing Set ....$15.00 and up

G.I. Joe ® Combat Medic Kit .... $25.00 **and up**
Jumbo G.I. Joe ® Action Pilot Coloring Book ..... $10.00 **and up**
G.I. Joe ® Action Soldier Coloring Book .... $10.00 **and up**
G.I. Joe ® Sticker Fun Book .... $10.00 **and up**
G.I. Joe ® Coloring Book .... $10.00 **and up**

Page 64
G.I Joe ® Pencil Box $20.00
G.I. Joe ® Jigsaw Puzzle .... $5.00 **and up**
Mess Kit .... $10.00 **and up**
Rare G.I. Joe ® Watch .... $150.00 **and up**
Child-Size Waterproof Poncho and Hood .... $20.00 **and up**
Bop Bag Punching Toy German Soldier .... $50.00 **and up**
Adventure Team Colorform Set .... $15.00 **and up**
Adventure Team Dangerous Assignment Game $15.00 **and up**

Page 65
Adventure Team Small Book Record Set .... (Each) $10.00
Large Book and Record .... $15.00 **and up**
Adventure Team Headquarters .... $25.00 **and up**
Mike Powers Outpost Headquarters .... $35.00 **and up**

Chapter 6
ACTION FIGURES FROM AROUND THE WORLD

Page 67
Takara of Japan
    Figure #1 .... $95.00 **and up**
    Figure #2 .... $95.00 **and up**
    Figure #3 .... $95.00 **and up**
    Figure #4 .... $95.00 **and up**
    Figure #5 .... $95.00 **and up**
    Figure #6 .... $95.00 **and up**

Page 68
Takara of Japan
    Basic Figure #1 .... #55.00 **and up**
    Basic Figure #2 .... $55.00 **and up**
    Basic Figure #3 .... $55.00 **and up**
Assorted Accessory Packs Small Arms .... $20.00 **and up**
Carded Accessory Packs .... $25.00 **and up**
Takara of Japan Assorted Uniforms .... $40.00 **and up**

Page 69
Made in Canada G.I. Joe ® .... $175.00 **and up**
Schildkrot of Germany
    Team Figure and Accessory Case .... $50.00 **and up**
    Action Team, Hard Rock Figure .... $75.00 **and up**
    John Steele, Figure .... $75.00 **and up**
    Tom Stone, Black Figure .... $85.00 **and up**

Page 70
    Action Team, Black Super Peggy .... $100.00 **and up**
    White Super Sandy Figure .... $100.00 **and up**
    Action Girl Ski Racing Outfit .... $60.00 **and up**
    Action Girl Underwater Adventure Outfit ....
    .... $60.00 **and up**

Page 71
    Action Girl Safari Outfit .... $60.00 **and up**
    Action Girl Parachute Adventure .... $60.00 **and up**
    Action Team Fire Fighter .... $60.00 **and up**

    Action Team Polar Adventure .... $60.00 **and up**

Page 72
    Action Team Medic .... $60.00 **and up**
    Action Team Wilderness Adventure ...... $60.00 **and up**
    Action Team Highway Police .... $60.00 **and up**

Page 73
Palitoy of England
    Basic Action Man Figure .... $55.00 **and up**
    Action Man Soldier .... $75.00 **and up**
    Talking Commander .... $85.00 **and up**

Page 74
    Action Man Helicopter Pilot .... $75.00 **and up**
    Space Ranger Talking Commander ...... $95.00 **and up**
    Action Man Soldier .... $65.00 **and up**
    Accessory Pack .... $20.00 **and up**

Page 75
    Space Ranger Captain Cloth Suit .... $75.00 **and up**
    Space Ranger Captain Rubber Suit ..... $85.00 **and up**
    Space Ranger Space Pirate .... $95.00 **and up**

Page 76
    Action Man Mounted Police .... $125.00 **and up**
    Dog .... $5.00 **and up**
    Action Soldier Engineer Pack .... $65.00 **and up**
    Action Man Indian Brave .... $75.00 **and up**

Page 77
    Action Man .... $95.00 **and up**
    U.S. Marine Corps German Trooper .... $95.00 **and up**
    U.S. Army Green Beret .... $95.00 **and up**

Page 78
    Action Man Bunk Bed .... $20.00 **and up**
    Special Operations Kit .... $35.00 **and up**
    Rifle Rack and Guns .... $35.00 **and up**
    Action Man Royal Engineers .... $75.00 **and up**
    Action Man British Infantryman .... $45.00 **and up**
    Mountain and Arctic Outfit .... $55.00 **and up**
    German Pilot Outfit .... $55.00 **and up**

Page 79
    Action Man Mountain Rescue .... $55.00 **and up**
    Panzer Captain Outfit .... $55.00 **and up**
    Action Frogman .... $75.00 **and up**
    Royal Hussar .... $65.00 **and up**
    Action Man Frogman Outfit .... $65.00 **and up**
    Police Motorcyclist .... $60.00 **and up**

Page 80
    Action Man German Armoured Car .... $125.00 **and up**
    Action Man Armoured Jeep .... $100.00 **and up**
    Action Man Helicopter .... $125.00 **and up**

Page 81
    Space Ranger, Space Speeder .... $125.00 **and up**

Chapter 7
CAPTAIN ACTION® SUPER HERO

Page 84

Captain Action® Figure ....$150.00 and up
    Captain Action® 1967 Promo ....$175.00 and up
    Superman Disguise and Accessories ...$75.00 and up
    Kripto, Superman's Dog ....$30.00 and up
    Outfit Only $100.00

Page 85

"The Phantom" Disguise
    With Figure ....$175.00 and up
    Outfit Only ....$100.00 and up
Captain America Disguise
    With Figure ....$175.00 and up
    Outfit Only ....$100.00 and up
Aquaman Disguise
    With Figure ....$175.00 and up
    Outfit Only ....$100.00 and up

Page 86

Batman Disguise
    With Figure ....$175.00 and up
    Outfit Only ....$100.00 and up
Dr. Evil® Figure
    Dr. Evil® in Suit Only ....$150.00 and up
    With Disguises $200.00
Flash Gordon Disguise
    (In Part) $20.00
    (As Is) $70.00

Page 87

    Spiderman Outfit ....(In Part)$75.00
    Lone Ranger Outfit ....(In Part)$75.00
Action Boy® Panther............................$30.00 and up
1967 Aqua Lad Disguise Missing Spear ....(As Is)$75.00

Page 88

1967 Action Boy® Figure
    Robin Disguise $100.00
Captain Action® Car-Silver Streak ....$100.00 and up
Jet Mortar ....$50.00 and up
Weapons Arsenal with 10 piece set ....$50.00 and up
Action Cave (Vinyl Carrying Case) ....$70.00 and up

Chapter 8
Ken® Doll and Friends "Everyday Life"

Page 90

Ken® Doll (1961) $80.00
    (1962) $70.00
    (1964) $150.00
    (1969) $60.00
Allen® Doll (1963) $60.00
    (1964) $150.00
Talking Brad® Doll (1969) $60.00
    Bendable (1971) (Reg) $55.00
    Bendable (1971) (Reg) $55.00

Page 91

Live Action Ken® Doll on Stage (1971) $70.00

Walk Lively Ken® Doll (1970) $70.00
Busy Ken® Doll (1972) $65.00
Busy Talking Ken® Doll (1972) $100.00
Mod Hair Ken® Doll (1973) $30.00
Now Look Ken® Doll (1973) $30.00

Page 92

Ken® Tuxedo #787 ....$60.00
Sport Shorts #783 ....$30.00
Campus Hero #770 ....$30.00
Ken® Doll in Dreamboat #785 ....$40.00
Ken® Doll in Casuals #782 ....$30.00
Ken® Doll in Saturday Date #786 ....$40.00
Ken® Doll in Terry Togs #784 ....$30.00
Allen® Doll in Sleeper Set #781 ....$20.00
Ken® Doll in "In Training" #780 ....$20.00

Page 93

Ken® in "The Yachtsman" #789 ....$30.00
Allen® in "Fun On Ice" #791 ....$35.00
Ken® in "Army and Airforce" #797 ....$60.00
Ken® Doll in "Play Ball" #792 ....$35.00
Ken® Doll in "Touchdown" #799 ....$35.00
Ken® Doll in "Touchdown #799 ....$35.00
Ken® Doll in "Ski Champion" #798 ....$45.00

Page 94

Ken® Doll in "Red Riding Hood Wolf" #0880 ....(As Is)$40.00
Ken® Doll in "Arabian Knights" #0774 ....$60.00
Ken® Doll in "Masquerade" #794 ....$30.00
Ken® Doll in "Dr. Ken" #793 ....$40.00
Ken® Doll in "Graduation" #795 ....$25.00
Ken® Doll in "King Arthur" #0773 ....$55.00
Ken® Doll in "The Prince" #0772 ....$55.00

Page 95

Allen® Doll in "Ken in Switzerland" #0776 ....$55.00
Ken® Doll in "Ken in Holland" #0777 ....$40.00
Ken® Doll in "Ken in Hawaii" #1404 ....$45.00
Ken® Doll in "Ken in Mexico" #1404 ....$55.00
Ken® Doll in "Campus Corduroys" #1410...................$40.00
    White Shirt and Red Tie Pack Set $15.00
Ken® Doll in "American Airlines Captain" #0779 ....$40.00
Ken® Doll in "Campus Hero" #0770 ....$30.00

Page 96

Allen® Doll in "Roller Skate Date" #1405 ....$20.00
Ken® Doll in "Victory Dance" #1411 ....$40.00
Ken® in "The Yachtsman" #0789 (With Hat)................$40.00
Allen® in Drum Major #0775 ....$35.00
Ken® in "Special Date" #1401 ....$30.00
Ken® Doll in "Country Clubbin" #1400 ....$20.00
Allen® Doll in "Ken Skin Diver #1406 ....$20.00
Ken® Doll in "Boxer" $15.00

Page 97

Ken® Doll in "Going Bowling" #1403 ....$15.00
Allen® Doll in "Fraternity Meeting #1408 ....$20.00
Ken® Doll in "Goin Huntin" #1409 ....$30.00
Ken® Doll in "Cheerful Chef" Pack Set $25.00
Ken® Doll in "Mr. Astronaut" $50.00
Allen® Doll in "Off to Bed" #1413 ....$40.00

Chapter 8 (continued)

Allen® Doll in "Hiking Holiday" $25.00
Allen® Doll in "Holiday" $45.00
Ken® Doll in "College Student" #1416 .... $50.00

Page 98

Allen® Doll in "Rovin Reporter" #1417 .... $35.00
Allen® Doll in "Best Man" #1425 .... $80.00
Allen® Doll in "Jazz Concert" #1420 .... $50.00
Allen® Doll in "Seein' The Sights" #1421 .... $45.00
Ken® Doll in "Here Comes The Groom" #1426 .... $100.00
Ken® Doll in "T.V.'s Good Tonight" #1419 .... $30.00
Ken® Doll in "Summer Job" #1422 .... $75.00
Allen® Doll in "Ken A GO GO" #1423 .... $60.00
Ken® Doll in "Time to Turn In" #1418 .... $30.00

Page 99

Ken® Doll in "Business Appointment" #1424 .... $175.00
Assorted Ken® Packs .... **(Each) From $15.00 to** $20.00
    Ken® Doll in "Rally Gear" #1429 .... $25.00
    Brad® Doll in "Town Turtle" #1430 .... $25.00
    Brad® Doll in "Groovy Formal" $30.00

Page 100

    Ken® Doll in "Play It Cool" #1423 .... $25.00
    Ken® Doll in "Big Business" #1434 .... $25.00
    Ken® Doll in "Bold Gold" #1436 .... $25.00
    Ken® Doll and Brad in "Shore Lines" #1435 ..... $35.00

Ken® Doll's "Breakfast at 7" #1428 .... $20.00
    Ken® Doll in "Sea Scene" #1473 .... $25.00
    Brad® Doll in "V.I.P. Scene" #1473 .... $25.00
    Ken® Doll in "Casual Scene" #1472 .... $25.00

Page 101

    Ken® Doll in "Ski-ing Scene" #1438 .... $30.00
    Ken® Doll in "Suede Scene" #1439 .... $25.00
    Ken® Doll in "Night Scene" #1496 .... $30.00
Malibu Ken® Gift Set "Surf's In" $200.00
Ken's® "Hot Rod" .... **$75.00 and up**

Page 102

Ken's® Wardrobe Closet .... **$30.00 and up**
Child-size Vinyl and Foam Throw Pillow .... **$15.00 and up**

Page 103

First Ken® Case (1961) .... **$15.00 and up**
Second Ken® Case (1963) .... **$15.00 and up**
Ken® and Allen® Case .... **$75.00 and up**

Page 104

Ken® and Allen® Dolls
    Display Only $50.00
    Display complete with Packs $200.00
Ken® Pattern Display $175.00
    Pattern Only (uncut) .... **$10.00 and up**
    Display Only .... **$50.00 and up**

Schroeder's Antiques Price Guide

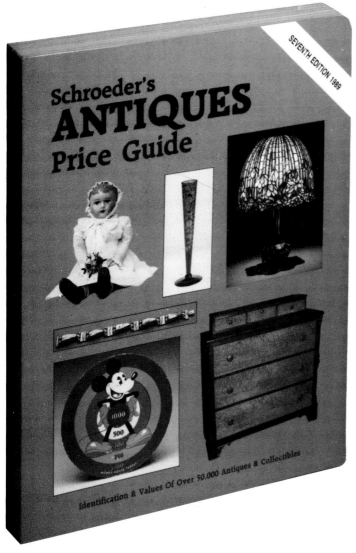

Schroeder's Antiques Price Guide has climbed its way to the top in a field already supplied with several well-established publications! The word is out, *Schroeder's Price Guide* is the best buy at any price. Over 500 categories are covered, with more than 50,000 listings. But it's not volume alone that makes Schroeder's the unique guide it is recognized to be. From ABC Plates to Zsolnay, if it merits the interest of today's collector, you'll find it in Schroeder's. Each subject is represented with histories and background information. In addition, hundreds of sharp original photos are used each year to illustrate not only the rare and the unusual, but the everyday "fun-type" collectibles as well -- not postage stamp pictures, but large close-up shots that show important details clearly.

Each edition is completely re-typeset from all new sources. We have not and will not simply change prices in each new edition. All new copy and all new illustrations make Schroeder's THE price guide on antiques and collectibles.

The writing and researching team behind this giant is proportionately large. It is backed by a staff of more than seventy of Collector Books' finest authors, as well as a board of advisors made up of well-known antique authorities and the country's top dealers, all specialists in their fields. Accuracy is their primary aim. Prices are gathered over the entire year previous to publication, from ads and personal contacts. Then each category is thoroughly checked to spot inconsistencies, listings that may not be entirely reflective of actual market dealings, and lines too vague to be of merit. Only the best of the lot remains for publication. You'll find *Schroeder's Antiques Price Guide* the one to buy for factual information and quality.

No dealer, collector or investor can afford not to own this book. It is available from your favorite bookseller or antiques dealer at the low price of $12.95. If you are unable to find this price guide in your area, it's available from Collector Books, P. O. Box 3009, Paducah, KY 42001 at $12.95 plus $2.00 for postage and handling.

8½ x 11, 608 Pages $12.95

COLLECTOR BOOKS
A Division of Schroeder Publishing Co., Inc.